LISTEN TO A SHAPE

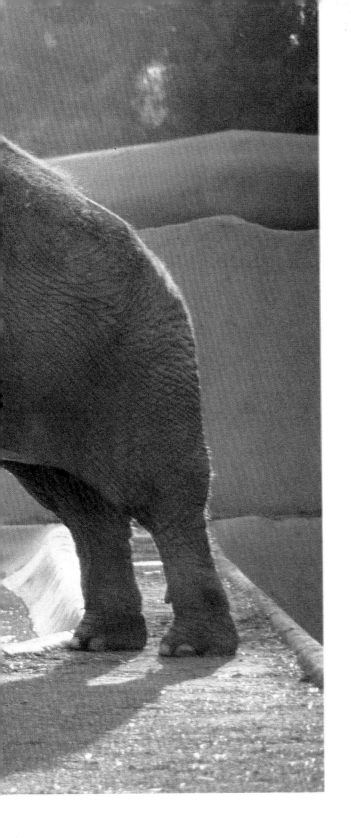

LISTEN TO A SHAPE

Text and Photographs by
MARCIA BROWN

FRANKLIN WATTS
NEW YORK | LONDON | 1979

TO KENNETH MALY
May shapes speak to him

Library of Congress Cataloging in Publication Data

Brown, Marcia.
    Listen to a shape.

    SUMMARY: Introduces such shapes as the
circle, square, and crescent and demonstrates the
many shapes found in nature.
    1. Form perception—Juvenile literature. [1.
Size and shape] I. Title.
BF293.B76   153.7   78-31616
ISBN 0-531-02930-1 lib. bdg.   ˙
ISBN 0-531-02383-4

ISBN 0-531-02930-1 (lib. bdg.)

Shapes talk.
Faster than words
        they tell you
        what is going on and
        how it feels.
Anyone can learn
        shape-talk.

ROUND curls up
    on itself.
Round things
    bring you back
    to where they
    started.

By the end
of the book
this fiddlehead
will uncurl
to be a fern leaf.

A snail can be
    long or round.
So can a cat.
So can you!

Spring comes
    up in a point...

    or floats
    feathery
    on the air.

One of the first signs of spring:
the skunk cabbage lifting its green horns
from the swirl of snow-melt.

A square city
in a hunk of crystal.

The world is made up
   of shapes
   like these
   that you can make.

Make a frame
   with your hands.

Make a square —
   all sides the same.

Make a circle—
all points on it
the same distance
from the center.

The spring sun
finds its children
all over the grass!

Make a crescent
like a hammock,
or the new moon.

On the sunset beach,
foam fanning in a crescent.
Day ending smiling.

A rectangle has
four right angles,
four sides, often
two one size and
two another.
This page is
a rectangle.

*This big bird is showing you
how one looks
with his wings.
His shadow is doing
the flying.*

Make a triangle—
three sides,
three corners.
Like some
butterfly's wing.

BUT
>wherever you drive a car
anywhere in the world,
this shape says,
"STOP!"

BUT
What shape is
the rain?

Through the spring sunshine
the April willow sprinkling
its yellow-green rain.

What shape is
a cloud?

What shape is
the wind?

*Who rolled these
tiny snowballs
for a
tiny snowman?*

What shape is
a flame?

Shadows tell
a different tale.

The straight branch
lays a shadow
on the curved tree
and leaves
a curved shadow.

*A fox is hunting
a water bird.
When will
he catch it?
(You can make
them both with
your fingers.)*

Can you see a bird,
   or only an old tree?
   Both shapes are there.

A miracle:
   Young things
   have inside them
   the plan
   for the shape
   they will become.
   So do you!

*This handsome caterpillar
eats the milkweed leaves
so that he can be
a handsome butterfly.*

*The little cygnet
already lifting his neck
in a swan's S curve.*

Some shapes say,
    "We look like something else.
    We want to join your zoo!"

This giraffe's tooth
is still chewing!

This knot of wood says,
  "Shall I chase my tail,
    or just yell?"

More creatures
for your zoo.

An ice turkey
gobbler for
your ice farm.

Wouldn't you like to ask this fellow
to come inside out of the cold?

A rare bird.

A dragon from
green sausage land.
("Delicious," he says.)

Some shapes side by side
bring you up short.
But they say,
"We're different.
That's why we look well
together."

Some shapes
are twins,
but you find them
in different places.

*The great flower floating
on the May dusk, unfolding
its petals like wings.*

There's a reason
  for a shape.

Playing endlessly,
  the sea waves
  push the sand
  on the shore
  into ripples
  like these.

The wind blowing up
  pushes the river
  flowing down
  into ripples
  like these.

Before the storm
the wind
pushed the clouds
into waves
like these.

The wind
pushes the sea
into waves
like these.

When marsh water plays
with the sober shapes of trees,
they begin to dance.

Water can
    take any shape,
    change most shapes,
    decide some shapes,
    change its own shape.

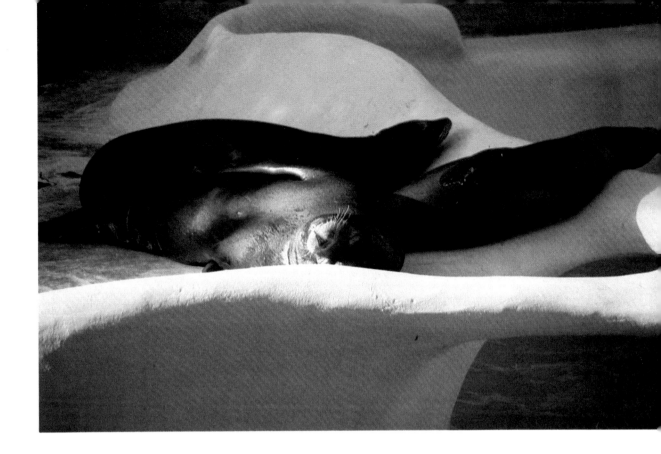

The seals and the fish
both have sleek shapes
for slipping through the water.

When winter water freezes,
ice can coat the world
in shapes that are spiky.

Cased in crystal now,
the river trees are waiting
for wind to ring their bells.

Take these shapes.
You can feel
    what they say.
    They don't lie.
You can dance with them.
They are your world.
They are in you.